GiRL TALK

How to survive

HAVING A
CRUSH

Lisa Miles and Xanna Eve Chown

rosen publishing's
rosen
central
NEW YORK

D1307400

This edition published in 2014 by:

The Rosen Publishing Group, Inc.
29 East 21st Street, New York, NY 10010

Designer: Jeni Child
Editor: Joe Harris
Consultants: Gill Lynas and Emma Hughes
Picture research: Lisa Miles and Xanna Eve Chown
With thanks to Bethany Miller
Picture credits: All images supplied by Shutterstock

Library of Congress Cataloging-in-Publication Data

Miles, Lisa
How to survive having a crush/[Lisa Miles and Xanna Eve Chown].—1st ed.—
New York: Rosen, c2014
        p. cm.—(Girl talk)
Includes index.
ISBN 978-1-4777-0706-7 (Library Binding), 978-1-4777-0720-3 (Paperback),
978-1-4777-0727-2 (6-pack)
1. Interpersonal relations in adolescence—Juvenile literature. 2. Flirting—Juvenile literature. 3. Teenage girls—psychology—Juvenile literature. 4. Teenage boys—Juvenile literature. 5. Preteens—psychology—Juvenile literature. I. Chown, Xanna Eve. II. Title.
HQ798 .M55 2014
305.23'5

Manufactured in China

CPSIA Compliance Information: Batch #S13YA: For further information, contact Rosen Publishing, New York, New York, at 1-800-237-9932.

Contents

MAJOR crush!

He's so cute it gives you butterflies in your stomach. His hair is perfect, his clothes are awesome, and his laugh is so adorable you want to die... But when he looks your way, you feel shy and embarrassed. In fact, you've never really talked to him. What's going on?

If I hide, he won't see I'm blushing!

Having a crush is exciting. But, sometimes, it can leave you feeling a bit mixed-up. Perhaps you think your feelings are too weird to talk about. Or you think the guy you are crushing on will never notice you. Or maybe someone is crushing on you? Whatever is happening right now, read on for some help...

GIRL TO GIRL

"A crush, to me, is when I like someone and think they are cute or hot. I know I am NOT in love and I wouldn't call a boyfriend a 'crush' because it isn't the same."

"I think having a crush means liking someone in secret! Sometimes, my crush is someone I just adore from a long way away. You can crush on someone you've never even met or spoken to!"

"I'm 14 and I have an ENORMOUS crush on a guy on a TV show. My friend told me that it was creepy. But it's not creepy. I just daydream about him and look at pictures of him and stuff."

Diary

You're crushing on HIM!

Stories from my life

It's time to talk about the cutest boy in the whole school – and possibly the whole WORLD – Chas Wallis! AKA Cool Shoes Guy. AKA The One who Sits Behind Me in Science. AKA My Future Husband... (well, maybe!).

I think about him all the time. His dreamy eyes. His blond hair. His cool shoes (obv!). I write our names together all over my school books with little hearts and arrows and stuff. Not my science books though – I wouldn't want him to actually see.

My friend Sophie says I should ask him out. But it's not that easy, is it? For a start, I don't think he knows who I am. And if I do try to talk to him, I will probably turn the color of a beet and start to stutter. Or worse... throw up!

Ew.

So, what do you think? Is it love or just a crush? And does it really matter if I never actually talk to him?

If I hide behind these books, I can stare at him for hours!

GIRL TALK

Real-life advice

Find a way to talk to your crush casually every now and then until you're comfortable around him. Then you'll have a better idea of whether you'd make a good couple!

THE LOWDOWN

What's a crush and why does it happen?

As we get older our feelings start to change. Having a crush means that you are growing up. You have feelings for another person and it's exciting – you will always remember your first crush. You can't choose the person you have a crush on. It's a feeling that just seems to come from nowhere!

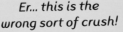

Er... this is the wrong sort of crush!

WHAT DOES A  crush

 FEEL LIKE ?

OK, admit it, you've been following him around for a while, you know where he lives and what his middle name is (because you asked your BF to ask his BF). Every time you see him your heart rate goes up about a million times!

It's him !

When you bump into your crush, you probably get a rush of feelings that make you feel strange. Do any of these sound familiar?

* **Excited** - your heart beats fast and you turn bright red.

* **Clumsy** - you trip up over your own feet.

* **Nervous** - you can't get your words out and you feel a bit shaky.

* **Shy** - you're totally tongue-tied and pray he doesn't speak to you.

Feelings of nerves and excitement are definitely signs that you've got a major crush on someone. Liking someone a lot and feeling excited about them is a kind of practice run for falling in love. You might not really know your crush and your feelings might have come as a big surprise, but there's no denying them, right?

THE LOWDOWN

Have fun, stay grounded !

Having a crush can be a lot of fun – especially if you actually get to meet the object of your dreams and you start to get to know one another. Just take care that your excitement doesn't make you do things that will make you cringe when you look back on them. He probably doesn't want a present of a giant, cuddly toy from a girl he met yesterday – if in doubt, ask a friend first!

If I buy him a teddy bear, he'll know that I like him. Right?

GiRL TALK

Real-life advice

Having a crush can make you SO happy! It's exciting to think that once you get past the butterflies you feel when you walk past him, and gather the courage to talk to him, you could have a lot in common.

Why does it happen?

He's so gorgeous!

Those "crush" feelings must come from somewhere – even when they are totally unexpected! So what IS going on inside that body of yours?

Body basics

Sometime between the ages of 8 and 13, your body will begin to change. You'll grow taller, your breasts will develop, and your period will probably start, too. This stage in your body's development is called puberty. But it's not just your body that changes – your thoughts and feelings do, too.

You might start thinking about boys and dating. This is what crushes are all about – figuring out who you find attractive and learning how to handle those feelings.

Oops! I hope I didn't say that out loud!

THE LOWDOWN

It's the hormones!

Ever heard the word "hormones" and wondered what it means?

* Hormones are chemical instructions that tell your body what to do.

* Puberty begins when your brain releases special hormones. Those hormones kick off changes in your body and brain.

* It takes time for your body to adjust to all these changes.

* Puberty can feel strange and you might sometimes find yourself getting angry, sulky – or experiencing the rush of feelings you get when you're having a crush.

Puberty starts between ages 8 and 13 in girls and 10 and 15 in boys. It ends between ages 16 and 19. Everyone develops at a different rate, so don't worry if you're not at exactly the same stage as your friends.

Don't even speak to me. My hormones are making me FURIOUS!

WHO'S YOUR crush?

Just because you've never met someone, it doesn't mean that you can't have a crush – even if the person is someone famous or someone totally out of your league.

He keeps smiling at me... every time I turn on my TV!

Crazy for... who?

It's not always the boy next door who turns your legs to jelly. It could be a movie star, a celebrity or even a teacher from your school. Whoever it is, the sensation is the same. You're crazy about that person for a while and just can't get enough of them, even if that means gazing at your math teacher for the whole lesson instead of working on equations!

It's good to remember, though, that a crush is just for fun, even if your feelings are real. Right?

If your crush is totally inaccessible, don't despair. It's OK to indulge your feelings, but don't let it take over your life. Your friends won't want to watch endless reruns of a music video just so you can show them the exact moment when your crush smiles to the camera – so don't make them!

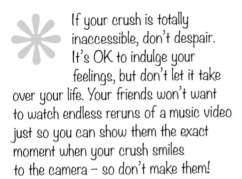

TALKING *Point*

Have you ever had a girl crush? Who did you like and why?

SHE wears shades indoors, so I'M wearing shades indoors. I don't care if I fall over.

THE LOWDOWN

Girl crush!

A crush doesn't have to involve boys! Having a crush on another girl is normal. And it doesn't necessarily mean that you're gay either. You can have a massive crush on another girl because you admire her, want to be like her or even want to be her best friend. Obviously you can't be best friends with a major celebrity, but it's still okay to have her posters on your wall or think about what it might be like to hang out with her.

COULD IT BE love?

Finding out that your crush is NOT going to be the love of your life can be painful. When you realize that your feelings aren't returned, it can lead to sadness and even anger. Remember, a crush doesn't always mean it's love...

Time for a reality check!

Love is something that happens when you really know someone – good bits and bad bits – and you know what it's like to be together. A crush is powerful, but it's not love and there's a chance that your feelings won't be returned. If you're upset because it didn't turn out the way you imagined, talk to your friends. They can cheer you up!

Did I send that message?! Er... yes, I did.

Keeping it real:
Don't be crushed by a crush!

If your feelings for your crush are making you unhappy, here's what to do:

 Get sociable!
Don't sit by yourself watching TV or listening to sad songs and daydreaming about your crush. Instead, get out and hang out with your friends.

 Get focused!
Don't get distracted and neglect your studies. Take your mind off your crush by staying focused on your schoolwork and your other activities. It all helps.

 Get active!
Go for a walk, ride your bike or go for a swim. Exercise releases happy hormones (remember them?) and will give your unhappy mood a positive upward boost.

 Get open-minded!
And the best way to get over a crush? Find another one! There's plenty of fish in the sea and you'll soon find someone else worthy of your attention!

JUST HOW BESOTTED
are you?

It's time for that reality check! Is your crush taking over your life – in a bad way? Or are you keeping your feelings in control? Time to find out.

This song always reminds me of him. And this one. Oh, this one does, too...

1. Last week, how many evenings did you spend listening to love songs and dreaming about him?

a) Five or more.
b) Three or four.
c) One or two… or none at all.

2. You go into a café and he's there! Do you:

a) Turn right round and walk out again.
b) Walk past him but cling on to your best friend's arm for safety.
c) Walk past him and say hi (even though your insides are churning).

3. How many times did one of your teachers tell you off for not listening today?

a) Lots.
b) A few times.
c) Just once – and that was when HE walked past the window!

4. Your friends are talking about a party you went to. Do you:

a) Keep quiet. You had a bad time because your crush wasn't there.
b) Ask them to keep a secret. Then tell them you wished HE had been there.
c) Laugh along. You had a great time, even though he wasn't there.

5. Your crush is a boy a few years above you at school. Do you:

a) Google him all the time.
b) Send him a message via his Facebook page.
c) Imagine what you'll say to him if you bump into him in the cafeteria.

Mostly As

Oops! You're besotted 24/7. Your friends have to stop you thinking about him because your crush is getting in the way of your life (that would be your REAL life).

Mostly Bs

Hmm... you're spending a little too much time daydreaming. It's OK to let your feelings rush away with you once in a while, but make sure they don't take over.

Mostly Cs

You know how to keep things in check. Yes, you're having a crush, but no way is it going to get you down or stop you from having fun with your friends.

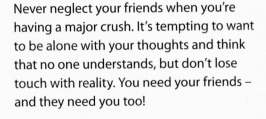

DON'T FORGET!

Never neglect your friends when you're having a major crush. It's tempting to want to be alone with your thoughts and think that no one understands, but don't lose touch with reality. You need your friends – and they need you too!

When a crush turns into dating

Stories from my life

You will never, ever, in a million years, guess what happened today. Chas asked me out, and I said YES! Which means we are officially together! My head is still spinning and I can't stop grinning.

After school I was waiting for the bus with Sophie when Chas and his friend James turned up. James asked Sophie if she would go and talk to him (all mysterious!) so they did – leaving me and Chas alone. He said: "I thought you might like to go to the movies on Saturday?" I nodded and must have turned bright red, but he smiled and said "Great. See you around," and wandered off.

Sophie ran over and whispered, "Did you say yes?" I told her everything and asked if James had asked HER out, too. I've always thought James is kind of cute. She said no, Chas asked him to keep her out of the way while he asked me out. OMG. How sweet is that? I am in heaven.

I'm walking on air!

TOP FIVE... worst things to say when your crush asks you out

1. *This is the best day of my life. I'm going to cry!*

2. *About time, too! I've been waiting months for this.*

3. *Are you sure? Can I have that in writing, please?*

4. *No way – I've just got to go and tell all my friends!*

5. *OMG, I love you! (Even if you're thinking it!)*

GiRL TALK — Real-life advice

Try to relax about your date. He asked you there so he obviously wants you to be there! Act friendly – remember, he might be scared, too.

TALKING Point

How would you react if YOUR crush asked you out? Do you think you could stay completely cool in front of him?

GETTING YOURSELF
noticed

You want him to notice you – but you don't want him to think you're desperate! Here are some dos and don'ts for when you're trying to get him to realize you exist...

What to do – and what NOT to do

DO smile and say "hi" every time you see him. (But don't do this if he is in your class and you see him all the time – you will look like a stalker!)

DO start a conversation. You could ask to borrow a pen or maybe his class notes. Then take it from there…

DON'T gossip about him with your friends and giggle when he's around. He might misinterpret your interest as silliness, or think you are making fun of him.

DO think of things to talk about, such as common interests, what you watched on TV last night or what you think of a certain teacher.

Woo-hoo! Look at me! You won't forget me now!

TOP FIVE... things you should NEVER do to attract a boy

1. Change your personality.

2. Send inappropriate pictures of yourself to his phone.

3. Date one of his friends.

4. Follow him around all the time.

5. Lie (about anything)!

GiRL TALK

Real-life advice

Be yourself – if you act out of character, you'll never know if he's into the real you! Find out what he's into so you can chat about it. If you're into different things, that's fine. You can talk about the differences!

WHAT IF HE ASKS you out?

So, he asked you out! The chances are that you won't know that much about him until you go on a date. You might not even have talked to him on your own before. There are a few ways that a first date with a crush can go...

One of these dates went better than the other one...

* **Fireworks!** You talked, you laughed, you had a great time. Then, he texted you to say how much fun he had. Now all you need to do is obsess about the second date...

* **Disaster!** It was obvious by the end of the night that neither of you felt a spark. Time to admit that you should just be friends.

* **Washout!** You thought you would have SO much in common – instead you were bored stupid! You could tell he was really into you though. You need to let him down gently.

* **Confused!** You had a great time! But you couldn't tell what he was thinking. Was he shy, or did he change his mind about you? If no second date is in the cards, you'll need to talk to him...

GIRL TO GIRL

"I liked this guy for ages. Then we went on a date, and it was awful. No conversation. I thought he was really cool, but it turns out he was just very shy and totally not my type – other than his looks of course. I guess you can never tell!"

"I had a date with this guy – we went for pizza. I think I made a good impression, but there was an awkward moment when he said he didn't like TV except sports and I thought he was joking! I hope there's a second date…"

TALKING *Point*

If you go on a first date with someone you don't know well, you should always meet in a public place. Why do you think this is? What are the dangers of not telling anyone where you are going?

"I didn't know if the date had gone well. I was nervous and he didn't talk too much. Then, the next day he texted me and said 'I enjoyed tonight. I never told you but you looked nice, too.' I guess some guys are just shy about saying things out loud."

It's not you
HE LIKES

Perhaps you got up the courage to ask him out and he said no. Or he told one of your pals that he only liked you as a friend. And then, maybe he started dating someone else… It's heartbreaking, but it happens.

It's not your fault

Rejection never feels great, no matter where or who it comes from. But there are ways of making it hurt less, and one of these is to stop "over thinking" and blaming yourself.

I'm going to write a really sad poem about this when I get home.

✳ Accept that rejection is a part of life – and what really matters is how you deal with it. Then, you can bounce back.

✳ Don't take the rejection personally and don't act moody in front of your crush's new girlfriend. This won't make you any more attractive in his eyes.

✳ Try to stay calm, keep your cool and continue acting friendly.

✳ Remember: you can't change someone else's feelings, but you can change your own.

Keeping it real:

How to get over your crush!

☑ **Look for his flaws!** Think of reasons why you wouldn't want to date him anyway. He must have some bad points – even if it's just his friends or his gross shoes.

☑ **Don't try to forget about him.** Instead act like he is just a friend. It will be harder to keep him as a "perfect" person in your head when you get to know him close up.

☑ **Find other interests.** So you were following his soccer team and watching his fave TV shows? Maybe it's time to stop and do stuff that YOU like!

☑ **Look out for other guys.** The quickest way to get over a crush is to fall for someone else. And you never know, your new crush might like you back...

☑ **If all else fails...** just give it time. You may think right now that you will never get over this but you will. Promise.

Time to find a different soccer team to support....

TALKING matters

It's important to make a good impression on your first date. After all, you've been crushing on this guy for ages. If things go well, this could be the beginning of your very own fairy tale...

Time to cringe!

It's very easy to do silly things when you're around someone you really like, and it's also easy to make a bad impression due to nerves. So try to think before you speak. It's very common to look back on a date and think, "Why did I have to say THAT?!"

Ground, swallow me up right now!

TOP FIVE... ways to make a bad impression on a date

1. *Show up late.*

2. *Talk all the time – without letting him speak.*

3. *Wear high heels and a dress – when he's taking you hiking.*

4. *Text your friends the whole time.*

5. *Moan about his friends.*

No, this date is not going well...

You don't have to pretend to like everything he does. Instead, just try to be natural and friendly. Here are some top tips!

* **Don't** talk about your ex and how much you hate him.

* **Don't** forget to ask questions. Boys like to talk, too!

* **Don't** talk about how much you like a certain celebrity.

* **Don't** let on that you talk about him to your friends.

* **Don't** let on that you have been "stalking" him for months.

GIRL TALK

Real-life advice

He's likely to be just as nervous as you are – even if you don't realize it – so he'll probably say things he didn't mean to as well. Try to relax in his company – after all, you're there to have fun!

DOES YOUR CRUSH
like you back?

So, do you think there's a tiny chance that your crush likes you back? Answer the questions and follow the arrows to find out.

START HERE!

Does he smile when he sees you?
NO
YES

Has he ever complimented you on your look?
YES
NO

Does he laugh at your jokes? Even the bad ones?
NO
YES

Does he notice when you're not in the group?
YES
NO

Does he seem nervous when he's around you?
YES
NO

Has he ever asked your friends questions about you?
YES
NO

Does he ever touch you on the shoulder or arm when you talk?

YES

NO

Has he ever asked you to hang out?

YES

NO

YES

If he makes a joke does he look to see if you laughed?

NO

NO

Has he ever asked your advice about other girls?

YES

BLOSSOMING ROMANCE

He's definitely noticed you – and it looks like you've made a good impression. Time for you two to get closer!

GROWING TOGETHER

He likes you, but it may be just as a friend. There's only one way to find out... Ask him (casually) if he'd like to hang out sometime!

BUDDING FRIENDSHIP

Hmm. It's possible he hasn't noticed how awesome you are yet! Time to turn up your smile a notch!

When HE'S crushing on you!

Stories from my life

Sooo, yesterday afternoon, I went to the cinema with Chas. I spent the whole morning working out what to wear – and nearly cried when I found out my mom had washed my jeans. They were too wet to put on, so I had to wear my second-favorite jeans. But I texted a photo to Sophie, and she said I looked hot.

Sadly, the date was the exact opposite of hot! It turns out that it is really hard trying to talk to Chas. He just says "yes" and "no" to all your questions. He didn't ask me anything. He didn't even like the movie, plus he didn't share his popcorn!

Deal breaker.

I phoned Sophie and told her everything – and she told me something crazy. James has a crush on me and was jealous of my date with Chas. That's James-who-I-think-is-cute, yeah? No WAY!

The date was a dud, dude!

TOP FIVE... signs that he is interested!

1. He asks about your love life, or if you are seeing anyone.

2. He brings up things that you have told him.

3. He touches you on the arm or shoulder to make a point.

4. He texts you or messages you on Facebook for no real reason.

5. He uses your name when he talks to you.

The date was great!

I really like her...

... and I kind of like him, too!

YOU'RE THE crush!

By now, you should have a pretty good idea of how to handle yourself when you've got a crush on someone. But what if YOU'RE the object of someone's devoted attention? How do you handle that?

He's looking at you!

First he smiles at you in class and then he's always next to you in the lunch lines. And your best friend says he's got a crush on you! You think she's right, but what do you do about it?

OMG, he is so cute. Is he looking at me? I can't look! He's looking at me, right? Is he?

If you know him already, then it should be easy to make up your mind. If you think he's cute and you like his personality, you might want to date him. Let him know you like him by smiling or chatting next time you see him. That should give him the right signal that you're interested in him.

If you don't know him that well, then go with your gut feeling. If first impressions are good, then say hello when you get the chance and take it from there.

GIRL TALK

Real-life advice

If you get the feeling he's into you, take time to work out what to do. Don't rush! If you're not interested, it's still a big compliment that he likes you. But if you think you might like him, too, how cool is that?

TOP FIVE...
best things about being asked out

1 *Hearing your friends say he's great – and they're a bit jealous!*

2 *Choosing what to wear – your best friend needs to advise!*

3 *Looking forward to the event – the anticipation is almost killing you!*

4 *Holding his hand for the first time – he's so gorge!*

5 *Knowing that he has a bit of a crush on you, too. Awesome!*

HE'S NOT
the one

She's perfect!

He's awful!

What if the guy who keeps following you to the lunch line is NOT giving you the same fizzy feelings as you're obviously giving him? This can be a tricky situation to handle, but here are some tips...

Don't get nervous

The worst thing to do in this situation is get nervous and keep chatting with a guy who's besotted with you, just because you can't get rid of him. He might think you've got a crush on him, too.

The best way to put him off is to be polite but not over-friendly. If he does pluck up the courage to speak to you, answer but make an excuse to leave quickly – like your best friend is waiting for you and you're late!

If it comes to the crunch and he asks you out, let him down gently and try not to hurt his feelings.

TOP FIVE... reasons NOT to date someone

1. *He's really good looking but also incredibly boring!*

2. *You're good friends – and you don't want to ruin that.*

3. *You just want a boyfriend – anyone will do!*

4. *You feel sorry for him and can't bear to turn him down.*

5. *You've been on a date with him before – and it was terrible!*

TALKING *Point*

Have you ever agreed to go on a date with someone and then instantly wished you hadn't? What went wrong?

We had absolutely nothing to talk about – so we just admired the view for a while.

Crush...
OR OBSESSION?

The emotions that people feel when they are having a crush can be pretty strong. Sometimes they can tip over from being fun and light-hearted into something that causes a big problem. You might need to find someone to help...

Moms know best... well, they think they do! (They probably do!)

What if a boy is obsessed with me?

If a boy is following you around, calling or texting you all the time and it's becoming a nuisance, then it's time to make him stop. First you need to ask him to do just that.

✳ Talk to him or text him back and tell him to stop contacting you. If he carries on, then you need to tell your parents or find another trusted adult to help you.

✳ And the same definitely goes for you, too. If you're having a crush and it's turning into an obsession, then it's time to pull back.

He sat next to me in geography. But – er – he doesn't take geography...

THE LOWDOWN

Upsetting messages? Don't put up with it.

What if I feel scared?

The definition of an obsession is a persistent idea of emotion that is often unreasonable – that is, NOT connected to reality.

An obsession can sometimes make people do things that are wrong. If you ever feel scared or threatened by someone's behavior toward you, for instance if they start leaving you nasty messages, then you must tell an adult right away. Don't worry about getting the other person into trouble. It just needs to stop.

HOW GOOD ARE YOU AT
saying no?

It's not always easy to stand up for yourself. Find out how good you are at saying the big N. O. Then you'll know what to do when you're asked out by a guy you don't want to date! Answer the questions then check the panel to add up your points.

He just didn't seem my type...

1. Your friend's younger brother has a crush on you and asks you out. Do you:
a) *Say you don't think you're quite right for each other and let him down gently.*
b) *Say yes – you don't want to upset him.*
c) *Say "Absolutely no way – are you joking?"*

2. You need to study but your friends want to watch a movie at your house. Do you:
a) *Put them off and tell them they can come tomorrow instead.*
b) *Tell them OK – and ask your mom if you can all have pizza.*
c) *Get really stressed and tell them to go away.*

3. Your best friend is desperate to go to a dance class but you don't want to. Do you:

a) Tell her that it's not your thing and suggest that she asks someone else instead.

b) Fall out with her over it – she should know you hate stuff like that.

c) Change the subject every time she mentions it.

4. The editor of your school mag wants you to help out but you don't have time. Do you:

a) Say no and tell her she's crazy if she thinks you can meet that deadline.

b) Say no, but tell her you'll write for the next issue if she gives you more notice.

c) Say yes and stay up late to try to finish it on time.

5. Your boyfriend always calls late at night and your parents hate it! Do you:

a) Argue with him – and then with your parents.

b) Take his calls anyway, hope your parents don't notice, then feel guilty about it.

c) Explain the problem to him and ask him not to call after 9 PM.

ADD UP YOUR POINTS!

1. a = 2 points; b = 1 point; c = 3 points
2. a = 1 point; b = 2 points; c = 3 points
3. a = 2 points; b = 3 points; c = 1 points
4. a = 3 points; b = 2 points; c = 1 point
5. a = 3 points; b = 1 point; c = 2 points

5-7 points

You're afraid of upsetting people, which is understandable. Practice saying no in front of the mirror. Otherwise you might end up on a terrible date with someone you don't really like.

8-12 points

You're great at saying no tactfully. You draw the line when you know that something is wrong for you – and people will appreciate that. It's good to have a few ways of saying no nicely!

13-15 points

Oops, you have no problem in saying no, but you might tread on a few people's toes along the way. Lighten up a little! No one likes being rejected harshly.

Boy talk
FROM HIS POINT OF VIEW

Boys get crushes too! For a boy, having a crush on a girl means that he worries more about his hair and clothes when he knows he is going to see her, spends time daydreaming about her and he gets those nervous butterflies – just like you do!

I should be studying, but I can't stop thinking about her...

BOYS SAY...

"There's this girl at my school, and she's really pretty. I want to talk to her, but she always sits with her friends and I am way too shy to talk to her when they are around. I'm always wondering – how do I find a time to talk to her on her own?"

"I like this girl a lot – I see her around because she's friends with my friend. She's given me a stupid nickname – Cart Man – because I bumped into her in the supermarket a couple of times. Does this mean she likes me? Or does she think I'm stalking her?"

"I never know what to say to a cute girl I have a crush on. I get nervous and any ideas for conversation that I have just disappear out of my head! My friends make fun of me about this – and that makes it even worse."

HEALTHY you!

It's important to keep your body healthy, and it's important to keep your mind and emotions healthy, too. If you're worried about anything, it can affect your physical health, too, so it's best to get it checked out.

Body and mind

If you have a crush and you're worried about your feelings, you could be making yourself unwell. Here are the important things to remember about staying healthy – and happy!

* **Get some sleep** - you need eight or nine hours a night, especially on a school night.

* **Eat healthily** - have regular meals and definitely don't skip breakfast!

* **Take some exercise** - go for a long walk, a swim or a bike ride. Exercise makes you feel happier, as well as being good for your body!

* **Spend time with your best friends** - talking will cheer you up, take your mind off your crush and blow away those worries.

THE LOWDOWN

Could I be gay?

Lots of young women wonder about whether they might be gay (a lesbian) or bisexual. Lesbians are women who are attracted to women and bisexual (bi) people are those who are attracted to both men and women.

If you have a crush on another girl, sometimes that's just what it is – a crush. But if you find yourself sexually attracted to girls and those feelings continue, then you could be gay or bi. There is nothing wrong with either of those things.

Part of growing up is learning about yourself and it can take time to discover how you really feel. So try to be patient with yourself and follow your natural feelings. Don't worry – it should get easier!

Some girls date boys for a while before they realize that they are interested in girls. It can be a shock for some, whereas others may feel like they always knew it.

FAQs

Q **I have a crush on my teacher. What can I do?**

A *Lots of people have crushes on their teachers. It's totally normal. But doing anything about it is not a good idea. Crushing on a teacher from afar and talking to your friends about it is fine, but if you start sending love notes or flirting, you will embarrass yourself – and your teacher. It is illegal for a teacher to have a relationship with a pupil. He or she is in a position of trust and would be breaking the law.*

Q **My friend told my crush that I like him. I don't want to go to school tomorrow in case I see him! I'm so embarrassed.**

A *Your friend may have been trying to help – or she may have been causing trouble. Either way, tell her that you feel embarrassed by what she has done, and would prefer it if she kept your personal feelings private in future. Even if your crush doesn't like you in the same way that you like him, he is bound to feel flattered. So don't worry too much, and just act cool. You never know, he might ask you out!*

Q **My friend is dating my crush. She didn't know I liked him. How do I deal?**

A *It's understandable that you feel sad. But try not to let your friend know how you are feeling, as it is unlikely that she will sympathize, and it is not a good idea to lose a good friend over a crush. You don't have to avoid them, but if being in their company hurts, it is better to talk to other friends for a while and keep a little distance.*

Q **I am crushing on a celebrity – I don't want to say his name – but I can't stop thinking we are meant to be together, even though we will never meet. That makes me really sad. Help!**

A *A crush like this is based on idealization. As you only know the star from interviews, photos, and songs, you will not know what he is really like. The best thing to do with feelings like this is to try and enjoy them for what they are. It's normal to have these feelings – why not look online or join a group to find friends with similar feelings? It may help to talk to other people who feel the same way.*

Glossary

behavior The way you act and treat others.

besotted Feeling strongly infatuated or obsessed with someone or something.

crush Intense feelings for someone who may seem to be out of your reach.

devoted To be very loyal or loving.

dilate To become wider, larger or more open.

embarrassment Feeling a sense of shame about something that you have done, or something that has happened to you.

flaws Faults or imperfections.

focused Concentrating your attention and energy on a certain thing.

gay Interested in having a romantic relationship with someone of the same sex.

girl crush Feelings of admiration that a girl has for another girl.

grounded Feeling mentally and emotionally secure.

hormones A chemical released by a cell in your body, that sends messages to other cells.

obsession A persistent idea or emotion that is often unreasonable, and not connected to reality.

open-minded Being happy to accept or discuss new ideas and try new things.

period A woman's monthly bleeding. Every month, the body prepares for pregnancy. If no pregnancy occurs, the uterus sheds its lining, which passes out of the body through the vagina. Periods usually start around age 12 and last from three to five days.

psychology The scientific study of the human mind and the way it affects behavior.

puberty The physical changes which turn a child's body into an adult body. On average, girls begin puberty at ages 10-11 and complete puberty by 15-17.

pupils The dark circular opening in the center of the iris (colored part) of the eye.

reality check A time when you are reminded how things are in the real world.

sociable Being willing to spend time with other people.

Is it a crush or an obsession? Check out the definitions above.

Get help!

There are places to go to if you need more help. The following books and Web sites will give you more information and advice.

Further reading

100 Ways for Every Girl to Look and Feel Fantastic by Alice Hart-Davis (Walker, 2012)

Blame My Brain by Nicola Morgan (Walker, 2007)

Bras, Boys and Bad Hair Days by Anita Naik (Hodder, 2008)

Chicken Soup For The Teenage Soul: Stories of Life, Love and Learning by Jack Canfield and Mark Victor Hansen (Vermilion, 1999)

The Rough Guide to Girl Stuff by Kaz Cooke (Rough Guides, 2009)

The Smart Girl's Guide to Growing Up by Anita Ganeri (Scholastic, 2011)

Web sites

Due to the changing nature of Internet links, Rosen Publishing has developed an online list of Web sites related to the subject of this book. This site is updated regularly. Please use this link to access the list:

http://www.rosenlinks.com/GTALK/Crush

Index